PROJECT EXECUTOR
HANDBOOK

Conroy Ellis

Conflict is a growth industry, don't let what
happened to me happen to you

authorHOUSE

AuthorHouse™ UK
1663 Liberty Drive
Bloomington, IN 47403 USA
www.authorhouse.co.uk
Phone: 0800.197.4150

© 2015 Conroy Ellis. All rights reserved.

No part of this book may be reproduced, stored in a retrieval system, or transmitted by any means without the written permission of the author.

Published by AuthorHouse 09/09/2015

ISBN: 978-1-5049-4407-6 (sc)
ISBN: 978-1-5049-4408-3 (e)

Print information available on the last page.

Any people depicted in stock imagery provided by Thinkstock are models, and such images are being used for illustrative purposes only. Certain stock imagery © Thinkstock.

This book is printed on acid-free paper.

Because of the dynamic nature of the Internet, any web addresses or links contained in this book may have changed since publication and may no longer be valid. The views expressed in this work are solely those of the author and do not necessarily reflect the views of the publisher, and the publisher hereby disclaims any responsibility for them.

Conroy Ellis is not a lawyer and is not able to give legal advice. The contents of this book do not constitute legal advice and should not be relied upon in that way. This information is based on personal experience and provided for guidance if this approach befits your circumstances. This book has been written for information only whereby legislation can change at a moment's notice so information is correct at this current legislation stands.

About the Author

Conroy Corvin Ellis is a Graduate with a Bachelor Degree in Business Economics and PRINCE2 Qualified Project Manager. He is also the Managing Director of Clementina Management Services set up in honour of his late Mother Mrs Linda Clementina Ellis deceased that specialises in Estate Planning/Management for clients/beneficiaries. He also holds seminars on the topic and invites guest speakers to contribute on financial related matters that can affect the administration and distribution of an estate.

Conroy Corvin Ellis grew up in Shepherds Bush, West London, England and regularly travels delivering his knowledge across the globe. He enjoys travelling and music and writing poetry in his spare time when possible. He has worked for numerous companies both Private and Public and has worked for Department for Transport and Ministry of Justice in finance and project related roles.

Credits

To my brother and sister and relatives who support and believed in me, Anthony Ellis, Sonia Ellis, Leroy Ellis, Joy Modest, Leon Modest, Dean Modest, Suzanne Thomas, Michael Awoderu. Mrs Linda Clementina Ellis, (1939-2000), Mr David Samuel Ellis (1930- 1998)

My past and current colleagues and many friends who gave me advice that has made me a better person, especially Frankie Lambert for his public relations and marketing expertise that has made this book a reality.

Preface

Managing an estate can be daunting task without the support and knowledge of the legal system and processes. An estate can be rewarding for the heirs once this has been adminsted. One thing that all projects have in common, however, is their potential for success or failure and the promise that if you do it right, you accomplish your goal. I acknowledge that every estate has it own facets, oddities and foibles that may need a solicitor with significant estate planning as your trusted advisor.

Why You Need This Book

This book provides not only the information but project management principles and practices that can help you succeed in managing an estate as a project if desired. You can read the whole book or find a Lawyer and review the handbook together and discuss any topics and questions you have concerning the estate.

How it's designed

This book can provide assurance of the work of a Personal Representative/Executor or supporting the layman and appointed family, friend, or relative to maintain open channels of communication between all parties, providing governance and visibility of progress with support of a solicitor. This is a helpful aid with checklists and advice to control and address issues that arise when dealing with an estate.

Who it's for

This book is for the layman or experience person looking to manage an estate. You will benefit from this book as it provides the structure and governance of managing the estate as a project if desired.

How This Book Is Organised

The book begins with an introduction to estate planning background providing the information and steps in the process. It then proceeds to outline in a checklist format the project management principles and examples of how they could be administer whilst managing an estate in practice. In addition, providing further reading and website references.

Acknowledgements

This book is the product of my time, efforts, and experience of being a Layman Executor and Ligant in person as well as using source information from the established authors in the bibliography that can be used in conjunction for advanced projects assignments and scenarios. In addition it is also, in honour, love and respect of my late mother and father, Linda Clementina Ellis, (1939-2000), Mr David Samuel Ellis (1930- 1998)

This book is the brainchild of my experience as a Layman Executor and hoped that this information and processes were known and existed and available on my journey of bereavement and estate planning matters that could have been followed to make a family, friend, relative estate transition amicable and a better experience than my own. In addition, where possible giving you my personal insight.

Within these pages I apply project management techniques and processes to the legal process to solve a problem, and for individual person or a family going through the bereavement process as when a loved one passes away. Therefore, achieving an economic objective or desired purpose of a project.

Contents

Foreword   **Page Numbers**

Understanding Probate and Inheritance Tax 1
Estate Planning Background 5
Project Management Background 13

    1. The Project Approach
    1.1 Turn it into a project 15
    1.2 Manage the project 34
    1.3 Assess the project 36
    1.4 Closing the Project 37
    2. Objective
    2.1 Create a team 39
    2.2 Your Behaviour in the team 40
    2.3 Make use of team members/individual competencies 41
    2.4 Work Together 44
    2.5 Effective Consultation 48
    2.6 Listen and question further 50
    2.7 Give and take feedback 51
    2.8 Conclusion 52

Project Management Templates
Agenda 53
Project Board Agenda 54
The Business Case 56
Task Report 62
Activity Report 63
Estate Communication Plan 64
Estate Project Plan 69
Risks & Issue Template 70

Executor's lifecycle Process 71
Project Controls 74
Project Initiation Document 76
Final Budget 77
Business Benefits 78
Lesson Learned Report 79

Bibliography by Authors 81
Useful Websites 83
Project Management Glossary 85
Some common legal terms explained 93
Accounting Glossary 97
Index 99

Understanding Probate and Inheritance Tax

In short, Probate is financial proof of someone death and the Grant of Probate is needed to act for an estate.

Probate is the name given to the legal process of attending to a deceased person's estate. This word has been adopted by the public consensus as the umbrella term for all estate matters. The word "probate" actually refers to the type of legal document required to administer a person's estate, through the official process of establishing (or rather "proving") the validity of a person's Will.

The objectives of the probate are to

- To safeguard creditors of the deceased
- To ensure reasonable provisions are made for the deceased's dependants
- To distribute the balance of the estate in accordance with the intentions of the deceased Will.

The person to obtain the Grant of Probate is the Named Executors in the Will to serve as the proving executor you must swear an oath to become an officer of the court to represent the estate on behalf of the beneficiaries.

A will is a document that explains what is to happen to your estate after your death. It is essential that you make a Will as soon as possible and keep it regularly updated if your circumstances change. If not, there is a chance that you will leave a situation where family members, relatives start to contest your possessions and fight amongst each other and fallout. The power of making a will is an instrument placed in the hands of individuals for the prevention of private calamity. Jeremy Bentham (1748-1832)

The Will, which is of course the legal document used to determine how a person's property is divided after their death, is a big part of the estate plan, although there are also other considerations. However, the Will is one of the most important documents and should take into account not only who gets what, but also who is in charge of ensuring the Will is carried out. This refers to the executor of the Will and is a very important decision. According James Grant, the formation of a Will which enables you to minimise your tax liability is of the utmost importance. In addition, this may mean that you could be liable for Inheritance Tax.

Inheritance Tax was introduced under the 1986 Finance Act to replace Capital Transfer Tax. It is a tax on what is known as transfer of value meaning transfer under the terms of a Will, or rules of intestacy which reduce an estate.

Therefore, the wealthier you become the more important this becomes. You will want to consult a solicitor or financial advisor in order to gain the appropriate advice.

The threshold inheritance tax is 40% on the estate after exempt transfer and after the current tax threshold of £325,000 (2013/14). The amount is increased usually each year from 6th April in line with the increase in the Retail Price Index for the year to the previous December.

Exemptions from tax

- All gifts between the dead person and spouse
- Lifetime gifts which represent normal expenditure out of the dead persons income during their life
- Lifetime gifts not exceeding £3,000 in any one tax year
- Gifts in any one tax year to a maximum of £250 per person
- Gifts in consideration of marriage
- Lifetime gifts for the maintenance of a spouse or former spouse/civil partner, children and dependant relatives
- All gifts to charities
- Gifts to political parties made within the year of the date of the death up to £100,000 is exempt

- Gifts to museums and art galleries
- Agricultural land, business property, historic houses and woodlands plus works of art.

Business Property

- 100% relief
- 50% relief on shares, land, buildings, machinery

Potentially Exempt Transfer (PETS)

Any gift outside the exemptions mentioned which is made within seven years of persons death will be included in the value of the estate. Any gift made more than seven years from the death of the person making it free of any liability for tax. This becomes wholly exempt once seven years have elapsed and the even if the donor is still alive.

Life Insurance Policies

This is a policy on his/her life and for own benefit the value of the policy forms part of the estate. This policy can be useful for estate planning as it is making provision for inheritance tax liability on the estate as a whole.

Gift with reservation

A person cannot give something away but still continue to enjoy it or derive a benefit from it. This gift will form part of the estate whenever it was made so long as the donor continued to enjoy it up the his/her death.

Therefore, when you created a will you need to consider the content and wording to be free of innocent estate planning mistakes. There has been instances such as Hastings-Bass' principle is intended to provide protection to beneficiaries from trustees' mistakes (including innocent mistakes) rather than merely breaches of duty. There also could be potential tax problems and consequences such as wording that can create an implied trust being possibly charged additional tax by its creation. I suggest a solicitor should outline and let the Will maker be aware of the consequences of the intended words that create such arrangement of that person last will and testament.

Spouses and civil partners also have the opportunity to transfer their nil rate bands which can provide a maximum joint nil-rate band of £650,000 on the second death. The prospect of a large IHT bill is an incentive for many to carry out IHT planning during their lifetime and reduce the value of their estate.

The IHT can be paid in full on receipt on grant of probate or over an instalment period of 10 years with annual interest accruing at approximately 3% of balance remaining on the outstanding charge.

The most obvious risk the Testator has when creating a Will is that the children or beneficiaries will deal with the estate in a way that is contrary to their wishes. Anyone should be caution about making outright gifts and exercise particular caution when gifting large assets or asset where there is sentimental attachment. The sensible approach would be to consider using trusts or other structures to shelter the asset from IHT whilst also benefiting their beneficiaries.

The current legislation has recently changed and the IHT threshold means the new rules do not start straight away. The new rules which sees a main residence nil rate band of £175,000 added to the current IHT threshold (£325,000 for single or divorced person and £650,000 for married couple or widower). It does not begin to take effect until 2017.

Starting at £100,000 it increases to £125,000 in 2018/19 and to £150,000 in 2019/20, before reaching the final amount of £175,000 in 2020/21. Therefore, you have to benefit from the full allowance.

Estate Planning Background

Almost everyone, single or married, has an estate. It consists of all property, including for example: A home, Personal Property such as cars and furniture, Intangible property such as bank accounts, stocks, bonds, and pension and social security benefits, and the face value of your life insurance policies

A will is the most important piece of an estate plan as it ensures that your wishes are carried out. It is your direction for the distribution of all property/estate after you die. This enables your beneficiaries to receive promptly the property you've left them as part of the estate plan. This ensures your business is not thrown into chaos upon your death or incapacity.

It can help support religious, educational, and other charitable causes, either during your lifetime or upon your death. It can be tailored to anticipate both mental and physical contingencies. It ensures every pound your estate has to pay in taxes is a pound that your beneficiaries will receive

An executor is responsible for the entire administration of your estate until the final distribution of the assets is made to the beneficiaries. This can be a complex and demanding task. Many people appoint a relative or close friend believing it to be a cost effective option and not really understanding the burden they could be placing on their loved ones.

In fact it can quite often be a costly decision as Executors require a good understanding of legal, accounting and taxation requirements, and if this understanding does not exist professional help may be required which can add expenses to the estate. Even with this knowledge there still may be the need for professional help.

Fortunately, good estate planning can help you avoid problems and it is not just for wealthy or rich. Everyone, especially those with children need sound estate planning to protect loved ones who depend on them financially. More importantly, this should give you peace of mind when you are no longer in existence but your estate will be for your heirs.

There are numerous risks that come with being appointed as an Executor. For example:

The estate administration needs to be commenced and completed in a reasonable time. If you fail to do this and the beneficiaries experience a financial loss, you could be personally liable for the loss.

As the executor, you will need to protect the estate assets. You can be held personally liable for any damage to property that has not been appropriately secured or insured.

You need to accurately determine whom benefits from the estate. If you make incorrect payments or incorrect distributions occur, you may be personally liable to make good.

You need to ensure that you have properly attended to the payment of all creditor accounts, including any taxation liabilities. As the executor you are personally liable to make these payments.

In the event of an ongoing interest existing once the administration of a deceased estate has been completed. For example, when beneficiaries of a Will are not yet 18 years of age, the Executor may become a trustee, requiring the management of assets over a period of time. This can be an onerous task and requires permanency and sound financial management skills.

You can appoint a Public Trustee as your executor to remove the burden from your family and friends and from your estate. They can administer your estate competently, impartially and with sympathetic concern for your family and beneficiaries. Executors can choose to transfer their executor duties to Public Trustee simply by signing a form.

According to essential Wills law, executors and trustee cannot normally charge unless the will stated them to do so. The office of executor/trustee can be time consuming and troublesome. Therefore, it is important that the charging clause included is appropriate.

Many clauses authorise a person engaged in a profession or business to charge for professional or business services. This does not authorise the executor/trustee to charge for time spent nor anything other than services of a strictly professional nature.

In my personal experience, I would not advise any Named Executor to take office unless a charging clause exists. My reasoning is simple only fools and horses work for free. I hope you have heard of The Little Red Hen Story which is the old folk tale. Your beneficiaries will not appreciate your virtues of your work ethnic unless they are put into a position whereby they have to pay for it.

Advantages and Disadvantages of having a Will

Advantages

- Protects the inheritance of children under 18
- Ensures that your wishes are carried out
- If you own a business, a Will protects your family against debt liability
- You can update your Will at any time
- A Will is a document recognised by law as the expression of your wishes
- Save on estate duty with proper planning

Disadvantages

- The court could appoint someone you do not approve of to be your executor
- Your estate Will be dealt with according to rigid and inflexible laws
- Your minor children's inheritance might suffer, since anything they are entitled to receive, will have to be transferred to the Guardian's Fund in a monetary form, where it will remain until they turn 18. This means that the family home would have to be sold (converted into a monetary form), which is quite possibly something you would never have chosen to happen
- If you have no immediate or close family, distant relatives - rather than close friends or a life partner - will claim the inheritance

Trusts are, in principle, a very simple concept. A trust is a private legal arrangement where the ownership of someone's assets (which might include property, shares or cash) is transferred to someone else (usually, in practice, not just one person, but a small group of people or a trust company) to look after and use to benefit a third person (or group of people

The person giving the assets is usually known as the "settlor" in the UK or a "grantor" in the US (but can also sometimes be called the "trustor" or the "creator"). The people asked to look after the assets are called the "trustees" and the person who benefits from the trust is called the "beneficiary". The details of the arrangement are usually laid out in a "trust deed" and the assets placed in the trust are the "trust fund".

One common misconception is that the assets in the trust fund are legally owned by the trust. In fact, a trust, unlike a company, cannot own assets and instead the trustees are the legal owners of the assets. The distinctive feature of a trust is therefore the separation of legal ownership and beneficial ownership of the assets in the trust fund. The trustees are the legal owners of the assets, but the trustees must at all times put the interest of the beneficiaries above their own. Thus, the settlor of trust can be a trustee, but they must still act in the interests of the beneficiary, not themselves.

The creation of Trusts started in 1150. A Trust can be inside the will itself called a Will Trust. There are various kinds of trusts but the main consideration with regard to estate planning as follows

- Trustee usually managed by two people, if you are the settlor you can also be a trustee. It's also a good idea to appoint an independent trustee like a lawyer or accountant.
- Often there is more than one trustee. There may also be more than one settlor of a trust.
- A trust does not necessarily end with your death
- The settlor can have the power to appoint and remove trustees. This is an important power that you can also transfer to someone else in your will.
- A trust doesn't necessarily end with your death
- Trustee have full discretion over capital and income

- Trustee makes the decision of who get what and when the time comes to distribute as they have full discretion
- Trusts lasts for 125 years
- Due to full discretion no beneficiaries have entitlement to the trust. Therefore, if a beneficiary goes bankrupt the trust is not at risk.
- No inheritance tax payable if one trust is below the threshold £325,000 nil rate band
- If an estate is above £325,000 nil rate band, the use of more than one trust can be considered called Rysaffe Principle that using a number multiple trusts up to the nil rate bad. As the Trusts unrelated and created on different dates this can avoid the Inheritance Tax liability.
- A Trust above the nil rate band are subject to periodic and exit charges due on each 10th anniversary of a trust and charges are calculated in accordance with the previous periodic charge.

Therefore the use of Trusts not just motivated by IHT. It is generation planning to ensure IHT not paid more than once on the same asset. The Trust protects assets against divorce, creditors, Long Term Care.

Start the Conversation

Every family's legal needs are different, but perhaps the most important step is starting the discussion. Talk to your family about scenarios that may apply to your lives and explore ways to be better prepared. It's important to know what the legal processes and laws for powers of attorney vary by country or state and continent, so be sure to research your specific situation.

By creating a solid foundation for your estate planning, from a last will to a living trust, future additions or changes to your family's circumstances won't feel as daunting when the time comes. After all, life never slows down. More importantly, and I am sorry to say you will die one day.

Estate planning should be regularly evaluated as a person's assets and interests will constantly change throughout their lives. Whenever a significant event occurs, a person's estate must be reviewed and a new Will made if required.

Examples of events that may trigger a change to your estate planning are:

> Marriage or divorce
> Acquisition of a new major asset
> Starting up or finishing of a business
> Acquisition of a superannuation or life policy
> Children marry spouses who are thought to be undesirable
> Marriage of children appears shaky
> Insolvency is imminent
> Tax laws are changed
> A discretionary trust is established

Project Management Background

Project management is the discipline of ensuring that the project objectives are achieved within the given deadline, constraints and so on. It includes:

- Project Planning
- Project Control
- Quality Management
- Team Leadership

Project management involves **Definition, Planning, Execution**, and **Closing** a project. In order to achieve a successful outcome, it is critical that you complete all four phases. When you define a project, you state the overall objective describe the desired outcome, and explain the scope of the project.

Planning a project involves identifying tasks and estimating the amount of time needed to perform each one. In addition, you need to list available resources and the costs associated with each one during the planning of a project. Once you have identified the tasks, resources, and costs, you can create a schedule. You can schedule tasks based on factors such as resource availability, time limitations and the relationships between them called dependencies.

Managing the execution of a project means monitoring the progress of the project by making adjustment when necessary and communicating progress. The initial plan called the baseline, can be compared to the actual events. The Project Manager can evaluate the project for potential problems and prepare to offset any negative consequences.

When closing a project, you mark all task complete. A completed project can be used for planning future projects.

Team Leadership

An effective project leader is often described as having a vision of where to go and the ability to articulate it. In addition, the ability to communicate with people at all levels is almost always named as the second most important skill by project managers and team members. Project leadership calls for clear communication about goals, responsibility, performance, expectations and feedback. A project leader must remember is that his or her actions, and not words, set the modus operandi for the team. Good leadership demands commitment to, and demonstration of, ethical practices.

Enthusiastic leaders are committed to their goals and express this commitment through optimism. In addition, a project leader must have empathy and presupposes the existence of the object as a separate individual, entitled to his or her own feelings, ideas and emotional history. We must believe that person knows what he or she is doing. Trust is an essential element in the relationship of a project leader and his or her team. A leader with a hardy attitude will take problems in stride. When leaders encounter a stressful event, they consider it interesting, they feel they can influence the outcome and they see it as an opportunity.

A team builder can best be defined as a strong person who provides the substance that holds the team together in common purpose toward the right objective. In order for a team to progress from a group of strangers to a single cohesive unit. Although an effective leader is said to share problem-solving responsibilities with the team, we expect our project leaders to have excellent problem-solving skills themselves.

1.1 Turn it into a project

Theory

A project consists of a number of activities that will be carried out in a controlled way with means to reach a unique result. A based method of working is only possible when a project meets certain preconditions. Ensure that the project has an adequate number of characteristics found in the ideal project.

The ideal project

- Has a defined beginning and end
- Is result oriented
- Is unique
- Is multidisciplinary
- Is complicated
- Is uncertain
- Is costly
- Is essential to those concerned
- Can be controlled from one point
- Has one principal or client

The specification of the project content is made up of two parts: the description of the intended project result and the plan of approach, primary activities or steps necessary to achieve this result. The result specification becomes clearer as the project progresses. It will be must concrete at the end of the realisation phase where the realised result is specified.

A project starts by determining what it has to produce. A good result specification is the basis of a good plan of approach. The project result must be determined beforehand.

The project result may be a tangible as well as intangible object. It is achieved by the following

- Determine the intentions, expectations and opinions of all those involved in the project
- List those part of the goals that can be achieved and the possible consequences if they are not
- Describe the relevant problems and bottlenecks in the current situation or those expected in the near future and, where possible, back them up with facts and figures
- List those part of the problems or bottlenecks that can be solved and the possible consequences if the intended contribution does not materialise
- Ensure that everyone involved regards the project as being sufficiently important, making it possible to push it through.

The project has to be determined and defined to turn the primary activities that have to be implemented to achieve a result and the sequence in which they are carried out. These primary activities are laid down in plan of approach.

I suggest create a calendar with all the estate's important deadline listed as milestones to be achieved and not to be delayed. You may need to discover documents both ones that were created before the person death and others that you obtain after the person's death that you need to start the project at the start up process of the Executor Lifecycle process. This is the series of steps the project will go through to achieve the goals for the beneficiaries

In short, the Will is the Business Case for the project and the justification for the costs, benefits risks and timescales, against which continuing viability is tested. In legal terms this is contract by the will allows the role begin and as the Project Executor once you have taking the oath. You are legal responsible for the day to day management, reporting, financial management and co-ordination of all resources and point of contact for the estate and beneficiaries.

In addition, as part of the initiation, the Project Initiation Document sets out how you can approach your estate strategy to reach your project goals.

An estate is about achieving what has been set out by the will maker as the last will and testament. Please note that there is also an element of achieving business value when managing affairs. It is the Executor role to ensure planned benefits and achieved to be distributed upon the closure of the estate.

The Project Executor should identify what the Will is trying to achieve and ensure a benefit management or benefit realisation approach exists to prevent a bloodbath or court action against him or her.

An estate can be a risky venture if benefits are not clearly stated in the Will. The project benefits can be subject to change control as the project progresses. The Estate actual benefits rarely match those expected when the estate started. This could be due to number of impacts on the benefits such as taxation, sunk costs or sadly the naivety of the beneficiaries understanding of the will.

Therefore, a Project Executor could include Beneficiaries to participate in decision making or quality check throughtout the project. If desired, allow a delegated authority to fully involved in the day-to-day progress of the estate.

PRINCE2 uses management by exception as an event driven concept, which ensures that interventions are made only when necessary. This allows a Project Executor to manage the estate without interference unless something is forecast to go wrong. The Beneficiaries can be kept legally and fully informed about the estate without the need to attend meetings frequently. In addition, the documentation deliverables can be presented to the Beneficiaries at Project Board/Checkpoint at a time and date frequency the Executor and Beneficiaries can agreed upon.

The advantages of using PRINCE2 in summary are considered to characterise best practice in project management. It can be applied to any project in any environment in any organisation. It is also highly scalable and tailorable to any project situation.

Therefore, a will can create the situation for a failing project to be stopped at the earliest possible moment as it is not continually viable for whatever reason. This could be due to contentious ligation or squabbling sibling who cannot work together in the best interests of the estate at all.

In addition, if consensus can be found a Project Board can be established. This allows managing the day to day running of the estate as a project in the knowledge that if necessary he or she can seek assistance from the beneficiaries or established professionals as a project assurance directly or by delegation who will be looking after the interests of the beneficiary perspective.

According to Robert Steinhouse and Chris West of Think like an Entrepreneur. Large companies are run by boards, where a group of people with complementary skills are gathered together. Options will be viewed from different perspectives before decisions are made. In addition, the process called IDEAS (INNOVATOR, DOER, EXTERNAL ADVISOR, STAKEHOLDER) is a way of establishing those perspectives using anchoring and a refinement of the four capability sets

1) Capability Set: Leadership to motivate and manage people

2) Capability Set: Administration and operations such as the basics of office management/project management

3) Capability Set: Finance and legal knowledge, the need for money watching techniques of accounting and the basics of property/wills/trust law

4) Capability Set: Sales, making friends and marketing and establishing people rapport

Therefore, the Project Executor could be working alone or in a coalition of family members or friends. He or she will have to create their own perspectives for him or herself. According to The essential wills law, the most important decision for a testator in relation to the appointment of executors and trustee is whether to appoint professionals or lay persons or a combination of the two.

From a project management perspective, The Project Board can approve a Project Initiation Document to provide a controlled start and represents the basis for committing money and resources to the project. It also acts as the baseline against which progress and success can be measured. It contains three essential management products which could be the Will as the Business Case, the Project Plan, and the Risk and Issue Log.

As mentioned, management by exception can be used to operate in the most efficient way possible as time is a precious commodity that some people cannot spare to be involved in the mechanics or decision making process. A report could be produced at a stage for circulation and commentary. This is a control check or fire break to check the ongoing viability of the estate as a project. Also a permissible deviation from a plan that supports management by exception is tolerance on time, cost, quality, scope, benefits achieved. This allows the degree of freedom and empowerment in which to manage a stage of an estate.

The Project Executor can also clarify to those involved that the project is finite and temporary. In addition, clear framework to ensure that the project is correctly started before large amounts time, cost and change effort are committed to it, and that when the project finishes it does so in deliberate way and therefore avoids problems of drifting continuously.

It is essential for the Executor to execute the Will in accordance with the law but what if the beneficiaries required a different remedy than what was proposed by the deceased. This is where a deed of variation could be used address the matter. More importantly, allowing the estate to address taxation consequences or an entrepreneurial opportunity that the estate can achieve via its alteration with a deed of variation.

As previously outlined there are risks of being an Executor. There are also risks when turning your estate into a project. A risk by definition is a concise statement of the event/scenario that might occur. Its cause is the specific factors that may contribute to the risk materialising. The effect is the consequences, both to the objective itself and the wider business of the estate. This would be defining the risk description. An Issue is a relevant event that has happened or present problem that was not planned and requires action to be taken immediately. In my experience, this could be an Executor attending court and to help a Beneficiary or defending a monetary claim against the Estate.

I would suggest you hold an open and collective discussion meeting to successfully identify the key risks and issues the project/estate facing from start up to closure using the Executors Lifecycle process and populate the Risks and Issue Log with the findings from that meeting. This will maintain information and support monitoring and reporting on identified risks. You need to think of a control action to address the causes of the risk and try to reduce the likelihood of it occurring.

As part of the estate planning process, at all levels, the identification and assessment of risk is required when setting objectives. Assessing risks at this stage is important as it helps determine where a successful outcome is likely. This is before time and money are incurred in the pursuit of the objective. If the risks inherent at this stage appear to outweigh the benefits, the necessary control can be put in place to reduce the level, or alternately the objective can changed or cancelled.

I would use a SMART test to support the effective management of risk. These test objectives as follow

Specific	Clearly stating what is to be achieved i.e. deliverables/products/outcomes
Measurable	Key performance indicators such as percentages, volumes, quality measures
Aligned	Consistent with objectives other such as beneficial interests
Realistic	Achievable but stretching within the given timescale
Timed	Included target dates/periods

You must define the Critical Success Factors (CSFs) which are aspects essential to the successful delivery of an objective. This can include the skill of the Executor, Creating an Estate Fund, and having Good Lawyer.

Identification and consideration of CSF will assist in identifying risks, as threats to these critical aspects are likely to represent significant risks.

Once you have defined the risk description, you need to assess the risk as follows.

Owner the person responsible for its mitigation and reduction, as well as overall

Management of the risk and the necessary authority to take action.

Impact were it to occur

Likelihood of materialising impacting the estate and beneficiaries

In addition, you could make three or five point scale for risk assessment such as follows

5	Very High	
4	High	
3	Medium	High
2	Low	Medium
1	Very Low	Low

The impact of the risk must be assessed on time, cost, quality and also the proximity. This is the time factor of when or the frequency a risk is likely to materialise.

The benefits of the risk assessement is that effectiveness and control provides an indication of the level of exposure should the control fail. The degree of exposure is known as Risk Tolerance or Appetite and by definition is the specific attitude towards risk taking, which dictates the amount of risk acceptable or unacceptable. If a risk cannot be managed to an acceptable level you need a contingency plan.

A control is any action, procedure or operation undertaken to increase the likelihood that activities and procedures achieve objectives. Control is therefore a response to risk.

There are four broad control strategies to manage risks generally as follows

Treat   Taking action to reduce the likelihood of it occurring or reducing the impact if it does
Tolerate Monitor the risk closely in order to detect any change in impact or likelihood.
Transfer Contracting out to someone better placed to manage it.
Terminate Change the activity that causes the risk or removing the relevant objective.

These controls used be used in conjunction with the SMART test to specify what will be done by when and by whom including a date when the risk is expected and controlled by mitigation. In addition, are the planned control strategy robust and clear to meet the date specified

You must also categorise the risk to understand its origin type as follows

Operational: Delivery, Capacity and Capability, Risk Management Performance and Capability

There is a risk that failure to deliver the estate on time for beneficiaries expectations leads to Maladministration. Or that you have selected someone who is not capable of being the named Executor as expected and does not have the confidence and trust of the beneficiaries. This relates to existing estate operations both current delivery and building and maintaining capacity and capability.

Change: Strategic Targets, New Projects, New Policies

There is a risk that your Executor fails to make the optimal investment decisions to make your share of the estate profitable. Therefore, unable to create decisions to pursue new endeavours beyond current capability.

External: Political, Economic, Socio cultural, Technological, Legal, Environmental

There is a risk that a law change on probate and inheritance tax, house price inflation leading to changes on calculation due to HM Treasury. This arises from the external environment, not wholly within the estate control.

Plan their activities and outputs
Decided how these will be funded and whether the plans are affordable
Get their plans approved
Put their plans into action
Account for what you have done

Pros of planning

- Helps us to be proactive rather than reactive anticipating, responding to problems and environment and economic climate
- Makes best use of scarce resources, prioritising, allocating resources where needed
- Monitor progress and exercise control
- Coordinating planned activities
- Consider different options available when making decisions

Cons of planning

- Plans can become a straitjacket and not sufficiently flexible in responding to changing circumstances
- A individual can become very focused on their own agendas rather than what is best for the estate as an whole
- Prepare/monitoring plans require the input of many people

The high level strategic planning translates into project plan for the coming year which will set what actions need to be taken in the immediate future to achieve the longer term vision. The project plan will normally be detailed for the next 12 months, with less detail for the following years. The project plan will revolve around the key areas affecting the project, including:

- **Objectives**
- **Resources**
- **Operations**
- **Economic Factors**
- **Information needs**
- **Finance**

The project will have set out its activities and priorities as part of the role of the annual budget is to encapsulate the objective in financial terms. A Business Plan can also be produced to show revenue budget covering the immediate next twelve months.

According Rudyard Kipling, The Five Ws, and one H, or the Six Ws are questions whose answers are considered basic in information-gathering.

Questions - What, Why, Where, When, Who & How	
Place:	Where is it done? Why is it done there? Where else might it be done? Where should it be done?
Sequence:	When is it done? Why is it done then? When might it be done? When should it be done?
Person:	Who does it? Why does that person do it? Who else might do it? Who should do it?
Means:	How is it done? Why is it done that way? How else might it be done? How should it be done?

When making a plan, it is easy to overlook fairly obvious things, which might only be noticed later on, when the plan is under way and things are harder to change.

To help avoid this, ask yourself, 'Do I know the answer to each of the following questions?'

What?

- What am I planning for?
- What is the plan supposed to achieve/alleviate/avoid?

- What does my plan entail?
- What options have I considered?
- What could go wrong?
- What will be my back-up plan?
- What do I need to put in place to ensure my plan's success?
- What will be the most difficult aspect of my plan?

Why?

- Why is this plan necessary?
- Why will this plan be successful?
- Why have I chosen this particular plan?
- Why will such and such a part cause me most problems?

When?

- When will I put my plan into action?
- When will I communicate my plan?
- When will I know my plan has been successful?
- When will I review the planning process?

How?

- How will I know if my plan covers everything?
- How will I put my plan into action?

An Executor can schedule the activities by week or months using the Task Report or the Activity Report in consideration of the resources available and the time taken to complete these activities. There are planning software such as Primavera or Ms Project that can automatically calculate linkages and duration of tasks if necessary. You are trying to find your critical path for the delivery of the project.

The critical path of a project consists of the tasks that affect the finish date of the project. These tasks are called critical tasks. If one of the task on the critical path finishes late or early. The project finishes late or early.

Before you begin an estate, it is important to be aware of which tasks are on the critical path. Then, as you evaluate the progress via Task Report or Project Stage End Project reporting, you can adjust tasks on the critical path as needed.

In my personal experience, this could be the payment of taxation or eviction of unwanted legacy tenancy to maximise profits for the estate and beneficiaries. In addition, the beneficiaries want their share and now and some people will go to great lengths to achieve their inheritance distribution. There is a Latin term called Sui Juris that means component to manage his own affairs. In short, give me what is mine.

According to Rudy Kor and Gert Wijen, The result description is the basis for an inventory of the primary activities that need to be carried out. Each and every one of these activities must be assigned to a particular phase. Phasing the project is necessary for planning and progress controlling of the actual project.

Only when the result of the project has been sufficiently determined and defined can thoughts turn to the primary activities that have to be implemented to achieve this result and the sequence in which they should be carried out. In addition, dividing a project into six phases will reduce even the most complex projects to activities and tasks that can be planned and executed with confidence.

1. The initiative phase consists of the idea and what the project should and should not be' all those involved have the same picture.
2. The definition phase consists of what the project result should be or do requirements/wishes/performance.
3. The design solution consists of the appearance of what the project result should look like a detailed complete solution.
4. The preparation phase consists of the groundwork and how the project should be made, what it will look like.
5. The realisation is the making or the carrying out of or introduction of the project result making it tangible.
6. The Follow-up is the using, up keeping and maintaining the project result.

How to achieve this according to Rudy Kor and Gert Wijen would be to

- Consider all the primary activities necessary for achieving the project result.
- Consider these activities in sequence, from beginning to end but also from end to the beginning.
- Determine the natural/logical order for carrying out these activities.
- Determine which activities could be carried out in parallel, possibly by splitting up some.
- Make sure that the description of each activity contains an active verb.
- Where appropriate, describe what the interim result of an activity should be.
- Specify the tools, materials, approach or method necessary for each activity.

Each project should have a remit or ambit and must remain within its stated scope. For example, an estate can be defined where it is simple or complex and the scope must be defined. This will prevent scope creep and if necessary use an estate planning resource for information purposes with accounting and legal advice when needed or necessary.

A **budget** is simply the translation into money terms of management's operational plan for the project. It provides the financial plan necessary to achieve those objectives and is a mechanism for allocating resources. A **profile** is the assessment by the budget holder of the likely incidence of income and expenditure during the current year. It is the run rate for an approved budget. It determines the monthly draw-down of resource to meet budgetary provision during the year. It helps the Project to manager cash, temporary borrowing and investments. The **forecast** is an assessment of the full year implications of the current year's expenditure and income. The **estimate** is the draft resource requirement for the following year

Accruals accounting by definition, helps to measure the value of resources consumed and income earned rather than cash spent and received in the year. This approach produces final accounts which more accurately reflect the cost of delivering project and help to smooth expenditure, rather than having big peaks and troughs caused, for example by uneven spending or major investments.

It is essential to have good financial information in decision making and sound accounting practice helps ensure that comparison can be made with confidence and that the underlying information has been prepared on a consistent basis.

Therefore, you can apply the matching principle, where resource expenditure to income within the current month and year.

In addition, there are different approaches to preparing budgets

Incremental – last year plus or minus agreed changes only, this is basing future spending levels on last year's budget may mean that important changes are not taken into account. Using last year's forecast would be more accurate.

Zero based is to start an entirely new budget each year, this is a root and branch review of the available resources.

In practice, the hybrid approach is a mixture of the two that enables all expenditure to be examined in the light of the project's strategic objectives outside the budget process. The hybrid approach is the one that most accountants would recommend.

Budgetary process

This ensures that the project manager is involved in formulating this own aims and objectives, in line with the overall project plan. The budget will be a major factor in measuring performance in the coming year and will enable the project manager to take responsibility for use of the money and progress towards key objectives

It is customary; before the financial year is much more than half way through the process for the next year begins a new cycle begins before the old one finishes

Set budget
Revise budget
Record actual results
Compare actual results with budget
Take control action if necessary

Therefore, the Project Executor is required to perform this task as part of the estate administration but professional assistance is advised. If contractors are used, ensure invoices are provided and if over agreed tolerance insist on a contractual agreement outlying the cost for the work to be done.

In addition, an accrual/provision should be created that as actual cost arrived there is funds to pay for them out of the estate accounts. This will ensure the estate remains solvent and the beneficiaries are not approached for funds during the estate administration.

The legal reason to monitor expenditure is for taxation purposes, as the Project Executor will be required to file income tax returns on behalf of the estate administration on an annual basis. This is for calculation of income taxation for the estate if running the estate as a business.

As mentioned, the **forecast** is an assessment of the full year implications of the current year's expenditure and income. The **estimate** is the draft resource requirement for the following year. Therefore, you will need to profile a budget and forecast if the project permits that is very important to manage liquidity. This can be done using the **Calendarisation Method**. This should reflect the most accurate estimate of the nature and timing of costs/income using previous year's trends and patterns of activity from previous years and historical data that could include non recurring items and know future events. This involves identifying seasonal fluctuations and ensuring that annual budget are allocated over a year in a representative way.

Making Budget decisions is not an absolute science and open to interpretation. Each person will prioritise spending slightly differently and make different assumptions and assertions in their decision making.

There seven steps to successful budgeting

1. Define your objectives
2. Define responsibilities
3. Gather the evidence
4. Decide what to submit
5. Test and Check profiling
6. Win approval
7. Live with the budget

Constructing a budget

Identify the budget period
Understand the basis of the budget
Understand the project strategic and business plan
Identify the objectives of the project
Identify the activities to be undertaken/financed in each period
Identify any income likely to be earned
Identify the resources required and available to meet the objectives
Profile the costs and income over the budgetary period

Budgetary Control

Accruals based on robust assumptions
Capture accruals data on regular basis
Check the actual resources against budget for each month and year to date
Identify variances and the anticipated under/overspends and the reasons
Manage within the overall allocated budget so extra funding are strictly on an exceptional basis
Prepare regular forecasts of outturn for the full financial year
Identify possible courses of action to remain with budget

Project Manager/Executor Responsibilities

Financial

- Prepare the accounts on a going-concern basis

- Sign the accounts and accept personal responsibility for them
- Ensure proper financial procedures are followed and records maintained
- Ensure funds are properly managed, with effective checks
- Ensure control of assets (Land, Buildings, vehicles, investments, etc)
- Ensure that issues of propriety, regularity and value for money are taken into account in considering proposals
- Make sound judgement and estimates on reasonable basis

The project executor bears legal/personal responsibility for these matters and expressed as the buck stop there. He or she has accountability for good corporate governance on behalf of the beneficiaries of the estate.

Third Party Responsibilities

Where contractors are used, please ensure that they are capable of the requirements to perform the work as instructed verbally or by formal contract if in doubt. If no contract is place, the obligation means nothing if it is not legally binding to the letter.

Estates responsibilities

In order to be successful and embrace change, I would like to highlight that change appears in many forms. One useful distinction is the difference between 'bounded and unbounded' changes.

Bounded changes, the scope of the change is strictly limited; the objectives of the change effort are clear and well understood; the nature of the problem is clear and so is what needs to change; relevant solutions are easily identified; and the change can be considered largely in isolation from it environment.

Unbounded changes, are where scope is essentially unbounded; the objectives of the change effort are unclear and there is little agreement on objectives amongst parties involved; the nature of the problem is not clear; indeed there may be disagreement over the problem is and what needs to be changed; it is unclear what would constitute a solution; and the change must be considered in the context of its environment.

Therefore, a major change will require the more change effort to manage the complexity and risk and usually many interdependencies of an estate project and operation. In addition, there will be conflicting priorities to resolve.

In my personal experience, an Executor never really know what he or she is getting themselves into until the work starts and it is normal to expect the scope of the role changes with time. You have to manage the scope creep by definition uncontrolled changes or continuous growth in a project's scope. This can occur when the scope of a project is not properly defined, documented, or controlled. It is generally considered harmful. This is important to allow the Project to be managed in accordance with the powers of an Executor and without intermeddling from Beneficiaries or being unduly influenced by friends or relatives.

1.2 Manage the project

The planning and progress controlling of the project needs to be managed by a number of elements, such as Time, Cost, Quality, Information and Organisation.

- Time: Have the beginning and end dates of the project been set and have the related number of man hours and materials been determined?
- Cost: Is there a budget for what costs and expected returns are?
- Quality: How good the result must be and how this is to be proved?
- Information: Are there any procedures for drawing up, releasing, changing and distributing baseline or decision documents?
- Organisation: Have all relevant organisation structures been laid down, project management, project team composition, division of tasks, responsibilities and powers and lines of communication? Does everyone know how decisions are to be made?

For example, as an Executor you would need to construct a management plan and use the five elements as control aspect to their desired purpose.

A budget should be agreed and approved for the entire project with regular (monthly) reporting against deliverables. A governance structure and project management methodology should be agreed at the start of the project. It would be wise to have regular engagement with the shareholders within the project or business to set expectations and capture requirements.

You must ensure that your financial resources allocated are directed towards the achievement of objectives as effectively as possible. There is a range of activities that fall within the overall description of financial management. There include:

- **Income Control** - ensuring that the income due to government is properly levied, collected and accounted for
- **Asset Management** – managing the physical assets of the project towards the delivery of its objectives in the most effective and cost effective manner, while protecting the value of the assets
- **Reporting** – reporting the financial affairs of the project accurately in appropriate formats to the various stakeholders/beneficiaries
- **Compliance** – ensuring that there is compliance with the rules and regulations associated with the legal and taxation framework
- **Delivering value for money** – providing services that represent and can be demonstrated to represent value for money
- **Procurement** – procuring goods and services for the project that provide the right balance between quality and price and ensuring compliance with the law and the other objectives of the procurement strategy
- **Internal and External audit** – Internal audit will be providing assurance that the processes and control in place mitigate the risks of waste and loss in the management of finances. The External audit is to examine the financial accounts of the project and provide a view as to whether they give a true and fair view. In addition examining the expenditure of the project to assess and report on whether it provides value for money.
- **Overview and scrutiny** – The role of an independent examination by an Professional organisation could be used for further reassurance

It is never possible to say precisely how long the administration will take because this depends on the nature of the assets and what arises. If there is a business to wind up or claims against the estate involving legal proceedings then it may become protracted.

From a project perspective, if you are managing your estate management plan, dealing with the risk and issues as they arise and performing the actions/tasks in line with the Executor Lifecycle Process and Estate Communication Plan. You are managing the estate affairs and the beneficiaries need not worry that the Will maker choose well.

1.3 Assess the project

The more information you have, the better the planning and decision making will be. The project needs to be assessed at intervals depending on the risks involved. An assessment of the phases and management plan is needed for attention to detail and usefulness and whether there are sufficient margins in place. The leeway for each management aspect as the controlling of progress is much more with the effectiveness and legitimacy of time and money still to be spent.

The Project Executor should review the bank statement monthly and update the income statement regularly. In addition, ensure the Executor Lifecycle process is being achieved task by task and to a required project plan and use the Task Report if required to report to the Beneficiaries.

1.4 Closing the Project

As the saying goes "all good things must come to an end". From a project perspective, a project can be closed once all task delivered and deliverables finished and documentation signed off. The acceptance process would be the essential steps of hand over. This could be property, cash, to the named beneficiaries.

I would suggest a close out meeting to review the project results achieved and use the Executor Lifecycle process to help with the project evaluation process. Lesson Learned Report during the project should be documented and distributed to beneficiaries. An End of Project Report can be established to show you have achieved all of the management stage to the end of the project.

As the Project Executor, you are responsible for the distribution objectives are required carry them out in accordance with the will. This may mean selling or put an asset in trust for the beneficiaries. Please do not be naïve to think conflicts of interests will not arise and unfortunately the estate matters being addressed in Court for resolution.

Therefore, I refer to the principled negotiation strategy to address the matter as the first step than using the legal system to address the matter. The key to closing the project should be based on achieving the directions of the will or using your BATNA to achieve what you want via a negotiation process if possible. This is the best alternative to a negotiated agreement and depending on whether it is strong or weak, the beneficiaries must make a decision on whether to proceed to court to enforce their interest or find a mutual agreement that befit all if possible.

A note of warning, a beneficiary can lose the right to a bequest. A court can decide in what circumstances this is appropriate. A criminal act such as theft or harassment of an Executor in pursuit of self-interests or selfish motives can affect your claim to what you are entitled.

Objective

2.1 Create a team

You need resources that can contribute to the administration of the estate and not hinder the progress. Therefore, I suggest that a lawyer, accountant and independent financial advisor can be used various stages of the progress and measured against the management plan of the estate.

According to Richard Newtown, tasks can be done by more than one person to speed delivery times and make the management of various tasks more manageable if complex. For instance, you may need consult a lawyer from overseas if the testator estate has international impacts and consequences for the heirs and beneficiary of a family.

When creating a team, the lawyer selection is crucial. Lawyers follow in the wake of the body of law as day follows night. Lawyers are rarely popular but as a skill set their expertise is value for money but to some expensive if you choose to take this adversarial approach.

The real problem could be argued that they tend to conspire often unconsciously to maintain the mystique of law, keeping their client in the dark or failing to explain the law and procedure or disclosing the consequence of a client wishes on intended action.

A good lawyer is one who not only tells the client what he or she will do for him/her and what he/she expects the client to do to help his/her own case. They provide reasons and explanations in plain and simple English.

If you are ligant in person find out the qualifications and experience and, if satisfied, decide if you would be happy for him/her to work for you. Please note, according to Edmund Burke (1728-1797) "It is not what a lawyer tells me I may do; but what humanity, reason and justice tell me I ought to do"

2.2 Your Behaviour in the team

According to Peter Honey, you are your own behaviour, you tolerate what you accept therefore, a project executor needs to use the power of the role by law to achieve the administration to the target model objective. Some families have hierarchy with brothers and sister using power and control via the moral authority of being the eldest rather than the most competent to undertake a role within the estate management. This must be resisted as the Executor is legal responsible for the success and failure in the eyes of the law as an officer of the court who has sworned an oath not the beneficiaries.

In addition, the use of assertive persuasion should be carefully managed. We all cannot get what we want, we receive what is bequeathed and more unless legally negotiated.

According to Susan Scott, honesty, active aggression is preferred to covert aggression. Silence can be used as a form of passive aggression. This is intended as punishment or an attempt to manipulate, to teach others that if they behave in a certain way, there will be consequences.

This backfires, as silence over a period of time regarding an important issue or question with regard to managing and eventually distributing an estate needs to be legally addressed.

Silence can let you think and plan each action step. Therefore, you do not make decisions or behave in a vacuum. Actions have consequences so you need to think in terms of who and what will be impacted and how and when.

In short, silence allows us to reflect on basic beliefs and particular issues before moving to options and strategies. It allow full participation for those involved and can be the best kept secret for generating family dialogue.

2.3 Make use of team members/individual competencies

You need to ensure that resources or a trusted advisor has the certain qualities and competencies needed to deliver the project. Neglecting to leave a will can likely cost the family left behind more money in court costs and eat up a more modest estate.

When a person dies intestate (without a valid will), the court supervises the probate process at each step causing delays in the distribution of the assets and additional costs. Such additional costs may include the appointments by the court of an administrator, as well as a Lawyer to represent the interest of unknown heirs. Any person appointed by the court is entitled to charge a reasonable fee. An Executor/Administrator cannot be dismissed short of evidence of serious misconduct.

The Executor should possess the following qualities to consider when choosing who will serve as your executor:

1. **Is the person trustworthy?** Your executor will be privy to all of your financial secrets: reviewing estate assets, determining your liabilities and paying off creditors, settling outstanding debts, and making distributions to heirs. Chances are you don't want all that information spread throughout the family or community.

2. **Is this person organised?** The person you choose will be in charge of a number of detailed tasks, both large and small. He or she will be making lists of assets, meeting court deadlines, making timely distributions for estate taxes, and more. Missing or being late for one of these many steps can draw out the entire process, costing your heirs both time and money.

3. **Is this person financially savvy?** One of the responsibilities of executor is to keep the estate viable (making sure the mortgage and fees continue to be paid) during the probate process. If you have investment accounts you'll want to ensure they won't languish and lose their value before they can be distributed to your heirs.

4. **Is this person compassionate?** Although probate can be a difficult and detailed process, it is at its core about the people you love. Your executor should have the ability to be caring and compassionate during this emotional time. Part of the estate planning is to help you think through who among your family or friends would be best suited for the job. If you have any questions at all about who to name, make sure to bring it up with your Lawyer.

In addition, the following questions should be used as a checklist. As ensuring your estate is settled properly with the factors in choosing the right person or committee of individuals whether layman or professional organisation.

The key in the selection of an Executor, young or old, male or female, is whether they have the executorial character, temperament, forbearance required to serve for now and many years to come if necessary for the beneficiaries.

According to John Thurston, anyone he or she wishes can appoint the executor even though that person may be completely undesirable as an executor. Anyone entitled to a grant of letters of administration with or without the will under NCPR 1987 can apply even though that person may have convictions for fraud, and be unsuitable as an administrator.

It should be noted that it may be that there is a duty on administrators to disclose facts about their past which may mean that they are unsuitable to be administrators. From personal experience, beware of the unwanted executor and don't let what happened to me, happen to you.

1   is there a choice of person? If there is

- Who has the most capacity to do the work?
- Who is the most reliable person with this type of work?
- What are the levels of motivation among the available people?
- Who has the skills or knowledge to do the work?
- Is it more important to get the task done right or quickly?

2 **What support is needed, and how does this affect the choice of person?**

- How much time or help from you or another skilled professional is available to support this task?
- How much time do you have available to oversee or manage the task?
- How much help or support will the different people who could do the task need?

3 **What is the impact and what is your contingency plan should the person chosen fail to complete the work to the necessary level of quality?**

- How likely is it that the person chosen will not do the work, or will do it incorrectly?
- Can you regularly check progress to decrease this likelihood?
- Who could take over or help deliver the task, if necessary?

2.4 Work Together

One of the hardest things to do is to talk your parents or loved ones about their future life planning. But if you don't, guess who could be dealing with it later? You! Here are a few ways to help make it easier on everyone and give you a jumping off point to get the conversation started. Good luck!

1. Have a Strategy: Approach the subject with care and sensitivity. Talking about future life plans and finances can bring up a lot of emotions. Have a strategy about how or when you'd like to approach the subject—in person, over the phone, alone or with others—before you bring it up.

2. Include Others: When it comes to wills and estate planning in general, include other family members. If you plan to speak with your parents about preparing or revising an estate planning document, for example, make sure to give all your siblings the opportunity to participate in the conversation. That will go a long way toward avoiding the perception that you are exerting influence, controlling the process or having the conversation in secret.

3. Get Informed: Before you can have a conversation about making a plan, it's a good idea to get informed yourself. Learn about the differences between each planning tool, what happens when you don't have a will or what probate is.

4. Be Open and Listen: When you broach the subject, take care to just listen and be sensitive to your loved ones' feelings. Asking questions is often a better approach than judging or imposing an opinion. Your goal should be to make it easier for them. Wherever they are at that time, accept it, and if necessary, come back to the conversation later.

5. Lead by Example: The best place to start is with your own experience. The more familiar you are with the process, the easier it will be to explain it and the less intimidating it will seem to your parents or loved ones. If you haven't made a will or living trust yet, you might consider making your own document, while they work on theirs, to share the experience and learn together.

6. Don't Push It: If you sense any pushback—stop and reevaluate the situation. Maybe now is not the right time or you might have hit a sore spot. Investigate it further to come up with a new approach that's less direct or intimidating. You might start cataloging their finances, for example, to focus on building the parts of a plan rather than the whole plan. Or you can start with a living will and health care power of attorney. Even if people are unwilling to discuss finances, most appreciate the value of putting their own health care wishes in place, and naming someone to implement those wishes if they are unable to do so.

7. Encourage a Dialogue: If it's something they've never talked about, casually bringing it up a little bit at a time over a period of weeks and months can help soften their fears or desire to avoid it. Then it becomes part of your normal dialogue and not such an emotionally charged issue.

8. Frame the Issue: Making a plan might not seem like the most pleasant task at first, but once you start, you'll find it to be a rewarding experience. Now that your parents or loved ones have an important part of their lives planned out, their future and yours can be much more harmonious and worry free.

Whatever you do, one thing is for sure doing nothing should not be an option. At the very least, encourage your family and loved ones to make a last will.

According Rudy Kor and Gert Wijen, content, procedure and interaction are three equally important aspects of working together in groups or teams on a unique assignment.

Content, is what, subject, facts/opinions

What must be achieved and how?

Procedure, is how the approach and decision making takes place

How the team will work together?
How meetings will be organised?

Interaction is who and verbal/non verbal, conventions

How co-operation will take place?
How we will react to one another?
The importance of consultation and buy in and enthusiasm
The need for clear support from all beneficiaries with spirit of cooperation

Without consensus, the project will die the death of a thousand compromises as the Executor struggle against powerful beneficial interests who may resist or seek to divert projects into their own pet schemes.

The vision has to clearly endorsed and communicated. The message is "This will be done in this particular way and we'll consult on and adapt the detail but the vision and principles are not in question. This empowers the Executor to move ahead confidently

Therefore, from a project perspective a Project Board Terms of Reference could be established to provide a core principle and behaviors of Membership for Beneficiaries as Members and Executors as the Chair as follows. By using the Estate communication plan and taking a step by step process can achieve buy in and support for the project.

Core Principles and behaviors of Membership

Members are prepared to invest the time necessary to gain an adequate understanding of project objectives, delivery activity and to carry out the specific responsibilities set out in the Business Case or the effects under the terms of the Will.

Members are willing to proactively champion the objectives of the project and support communications with their respective organisations or position of interest;

Members are willing to work collaboratively with the project team and members from other organisations to ensure that all issues and risks related to joined up working are identified and managed effectively.

Members are sufficiently empowered to make decisions on behalf of their respective organisations or position of interest.

Members will secure the resources necessary to provide input into the project as required.

Members will secure the funding necessary to deliver the project with the agreed timescales.

A project board is to moving the project forward and not an opportunity to influence one another. This leads to matters to be handled out of committee as no spirit of cooperation can met or found among all beneficiaries and their position of interest.

In addition, according to Richard Newton it is important as part of the success criteria to perform ongoing stakeholder and expectations management through the life of the project. A deed of variation could be used as a form of change control with agreement of all beneficiaries of the estate.

2.5 Effective Consultation

There is a saying that tells heirs that if you don't get along, your lawyer will become an heir to the estate. Therefore, I suggest that regular checkpoint meetings to assess the progress should take place. A prepared agenda and line items on it are dealt with according to procedure. This meeting should be planned, where everybody has their say, observing good time management and wrapping up discussion points, summarising discussion and drawing conclusions.

The cardinal rule is that everyone behave in the meetings, as raising your voice does not raise the power of your argument. It is the line items on the agenda to be addressed and no more unless it is any other business.

Avoiding conflicts does not resolve anything, it more likely exacerbate the problem. Conflicts, properly managed and handled can be a relief for all parties involved.

Therefore, an estate can have conflicts of interests between beneficiaries that will have to reach an agreement with to achieve a distribution of the estate. This can be addressed inside or out of court. I suggest family mediation as the first stop to resolve this matter.

According to Leigh Thompson gives two lists of preparation activities which lead up to the negotiation process. The first list covers activities carried out by most negotiators, but which are NOT the most successful:

Rehearsing your demands.

Pumping yourself up.

Making a personal pledge to yourself, or to your partner, to act tough.

Figuring out how to throw off the other negotiators or make them feel uncomfortable.

Preparing backhand compliments and downright insults.

Rehearsing phrases that include: "This is my final offer"; "My bottom line"; "This is a deal-breaker"; "Non-negotiable"; and "Then we don't have a deal".

Framing your offer as a demand.

Negotiation is a basic means of getting what you want from others. It is back and forth communication designed to reach an agreement when you and the other side have some interests that are shared and others that are opposed.

People have every right to participate in decisions that affect them; fewer and fewer people will accept decisions dictated by someone else. Whether in business, government or the family. People reach most decisions through negotiation. Even when they go to court, they almost always negotiate a settlement before trial.

People find themselves in a dilemma, they see two ways to negotiate soft or hard.

Soft wants to avoid personal conflict and so makes concessions readily in order to reach agreement and want an amicable resolution ending up exploited and feeling bitter.

Hard wants to see any situation as a contest of wills in which the side that take the more extreme positions and holds out longer fares better. They want to win but end up producing an equally hard response which exhausts him and the resources and harms his relationship with the other side.

A third way to negotiate is to decide issues on their merits rather than through a haggling process focused on what each side says it will and won't do. It suggests that you look for mutual gains whenever possible, and that where your interest conflict, you should insist that the result be based on some fair standards independent of the will of either side. The method of principled negotiation is hard on the merits, soft on people.

Principled negotiation shows you how to obtain what you are entitled to and still be decent. It enables you to be fair while protecting you against those who would take advantage of your fairness.

Principled negotiation is an all-purpose strategy.

2.6 Listen and question further

Here is a useful mnemonic for better listening skills:

L Look interested - give encouraging signs
I Inquire/ask questions/take notes
S Stay on the subject
T Test your understanding - paraphrase and summarise
E Evaluate the message - what is being said and how it comes across
N Neutralise your feelings - keep an open mind.

Active listening can be used in estate negotiation as there is a need to not damage the relationship between beneficiaries. If we are feeling listened to, we do not feel valued and acknowledged. The last thing you want is a beneficiary who feel upset and angry. This can cause a sense of disconnection and alienation from the people you need to feel close to resolve the matter.

Therefore, you need to give your complete focus to what the other person is saying. Please listen with an open mind, let the other person finish before you start talking. You need to reflect back what you have heard so that there are no misunderstandings. Please keep your emotions under control and do not interrupt or jump to conclusions. You need to look for the unmet interest and feelings or intent behind the words.

Active listening does not mean that you always agree with each beneficiary. It simply means that you understand or ask for clarification if you do not acknowledge what all parties/beneficiaries are saying.

Active listening helps to create empathy and come to an agreement. This can defuse a potentially explosive situation and enable you to find a constructive solution than deal with a court hearing to remedy the matter.

2.7 Give and take feedback

An executor can be thankless task but it down to you to achieve what is the best interests of the estate. If you have performed your duties with the utmost diligence you can stand by the decisions you have made. Your not the decision maker of the Will just the administrator from a legal perspective. Therefore, you carry out the statement of wishes of the Testator on behalf of the beneficiaries.

2.8 Conclusion

Money is the fruit of evil as often as the root of it Henry Fielding (1707-54) from my experience, parental influence is probably only one of many factors that shape our attitudes and beliefs. Therefore, if you never learnt how to share amongst your siblings as children how do you expect to share an interest in the estate when you become adults and suddenly expect to all get along in the best interests of the estate. As individuals we may not have the complementary skills to work together to achieve a desired goal or objective. Unfortunately, it is about self-interest nothing more and nothing less.

In order to resolve the issue court intervention may be inevitable and at cost and consequence of the beneficiaries harmony and an adversarial approach between one another. This will tear families apart forever and what is lost if we open a quarrel between past and present, we shall find that we have lost the future as quoted by Winston Churchill.

I would suggest you find a collaborative outcome, concession and comprise if it is in your best interests. Sometimes even lawyers need lawyers if you let the greed and entitlement get out of hand. Conflict is a growth industry, don't let what happened to me happen to you.

AGENDA

Meeting: Project Board/Beneficiaries Board
Date:
Time:
Location:
Ref:

Invitees:

....

....

....

....

....

1. Introductions & Apologies   Chair
2. Approval of the Minutes and Actions from the last Meeting Chair
3. Achievements this Period
4. Executor Update
5. Review of High Level Plan
6. Finance Overview
7. Key Risks and Issues
8. Plans for next Period
9. Any Other Business   Chair
10. Date of Next Meeting   Chair

Project Board

Date:
Location:
Dial in:

Attendees

Participants	Organisation	Title	Board Role

Apologies / Attendance not confirmed

AGENDA

1	Welcome, Introductions & Apologies	(Chair)	5 Mins
2	Board Structure		5 Mins
3	Project Update Presentation	(Project Executor)	30 mins
4	Business As Usual Update		10 mins
5	Key Documents & Approvals		10 mins
6	Any Other Business		10 mins

The Business Case

The purpose of this document is to:

- define the purpose, scope and output required
- to define the financial aspects of the project
- define the options considered
- explain which option has been chosen and why
- be the basis of a decision to proceed (including an investment decision)
- form the basis for the management and the assessment of overall success.

1. Summary Information

Requirement: The table below is intended to give stakeholders immediate headline information and allow them a higher level overview of the project. Populate from the contents of this document:

Key Area	Headline Information	Para Ref
Project Aims and Objectives	Brief statement on why we are doing this project – what it is aiming to achieve and why we want to achieve it	
The Benefits	Articulate the benefits to the client/customer (cost quality, delivery, capacity)	
Any investment	State any funding required, where this is coming from and over what period. State actual monetary costs as well as staff time/resources.	
Status of funding	State here whether funding has been secured, if not shortfall of secured funding.	
Project end date	Anticipated end date for project – including implementation	
Other relevant information		

2. Background

Requirement: Explain why the project is required, how it came about, including who and how it was authorised or mandated. What is the problem it is trying to resolve? How does it fit in with the project beneficiaries objectives?

3. Project Definition

Requirement: Fill in the following sections:
Project Aim and Objectives:
Brief statement on why we are doing this project?
What is intended to be achieved by the project?
How does the project fit with the main aims and key responsibilities?
To which Objectives and Performance Targets does this project relate?
To which does this project relate?

Specific Benefits required:
Articulate the benefits to the beneficiaries (cost quality, delivery, and capacity)
Are there any required outputs (new system or process)?

Project Scope:
What areas of the will it cover?
Are any areas excluded (people, resources, processes, customers etc)?

Project Method or Approach:
Will the product(s) be delivered from scratch by the Executor?
Will an external third party deliver the product(s) from scratch?
Will the product(s) be delivered from scratch with contributions from other external organisations?
Is an existing product being modified to meet new needs?
Is an 'off the shelf' product being bought?

Major Risks:
What are the key risks if the project is not undertaken?
What are the key risks in the successful delivery of the project?

Dependencies:

Internal and external factors upon which the successful delivery of this project are dependent should be specified

The nature of the dependency explained.

4. Business Case

Requirement: Fill in the following sections:

Options:

- What are the options for delivering the project?

Critical success factors:

- Critical success factors are those few things that must go well to ensure success for a project and, therefore, they represent those area that must be given special and continual attention.

Benefits appraisal:

- For the options identified what are the benefits
- Do some options provide the benefits sooner but at a higher risk?
- Do some options not deliver all of the benefits but at lower investment costs.

How will we do it?

- An internally run project
- External consultants/Lawyers?
- External supplier/contract management.

Affordability – ROI:

- What is the return on investment?
- Over what period

- Do we have the budget?

Achievability:

- Do we have contingency plans?
- Is the project supported?
- Have we identified the major risks?
- Do we have the required skills and resources?

Inputs from other areas:

- Procurement Impacts
- Customer impacts
- Third party
- Environmental

5. Project organisation and governance structure

Requirement: A project management structure is a temporary structure specifically designed to manage the project to its successful conclusion. Describe who is responsible for which aspects of the project. Define how decisions are made. Include SRO, board, Project Executor, PMO and workstreams. Where used include steering group, technical or specialist input including Quality Assurance.

6. Assurance and approvals

Assurance and approvals

Requirement: Define how the project secures approvals to proceed (including funding where required).

Define how deliverables will be assured before delivery:

- How will you know what you are delivering is fit for purpose
- How will you know that it is to the quality required?
- How will you know if it is going to be delivered on time?
- How will you know if it is staying on budget?

7. Communication and Engagement

Requirement: Communication is central to project management. The project's stakeholder management strategy aims to keep awareness and commitment high, maintain consistent messages within and outside the project, and ensure that expectations do not drift out of line with what will be delivered. The Estate Communication Plan is an important tool to ensure these objectives are achieved.

Stakeholders such as decision makers and the beneficiaries will need to be engaged at the out set to ensure that the chosen approach is appropriate and has the necessary support.

8. Project Stage Plan

Requirement: How is the project divided into logical stages? All projects have an initiation stage, a delivery stage and a post implementation review stage; many projects have additional stages depending on the complexity, scope and timescales involved.

9. Change Control

Requirement: Controls are concerned with decision making, and their purpose is to ensure that the project:

- Is producing the required product, which meets the defined quality criteria
- Is being carried out to schedule and in accordance with its resource and cost plans
- Remains viable against the project Business Case.

How will change to the projects objectives, benefits, costs, etc. be managed including how are decisions made.

10. Initial Risk Log

Requirement: A Risk Register should be used by the project to record new risks as they are identified, their degree of impact and likelihood, the chosen countermeasures and progress to date. The Register also provides a means of listing the management strategies adopted for all of the identified risks, and so facilitates the consideration of all of a project's risks and their comparative impact, likelihood or proximity at Project Board's discussions.

11. Project Filing

Requirement: This section of the document should set out the procedures for storage, retrieval and control of the documents (in both electronic and hard formats) used in the project.

Task Report

ID	Task Name	Duration	Start	Finish	Predecessors

Activity Report:

Period: Week ending

Activities / Achievements this week:
•   •   •   •   •
Activities Planned for Next Week:
•   •   •   •   •
Longer Term Outlook – including Risks, Issues, Concerns:
• There is a risk that if the estate is not managed the Estate Project Plan will be delayed and delivery timescales will be impacted.

Estate Communication Plan

Pre Will Objectives
Have a family meeting to discuss your will making intentions
Create an estate fund, even when a will is written and recorded, until the bills are paid, no one inherits.
Create draft will, Lasting Power of Attorney, pilot trust
Arrange pre-paid funeral plan, Purchase casket and funeral services in advance. Funeral insurance: Purchase a policy to cover the expenses family will incur if you cannot prepay.
Speak to Independent Financial Adviser and make sure all financial documentation are up date and relevant
Will approved and witnessed and stored with your executor with letter of instruction
Arrange Lasting Power of Attorney and Pilot Trusts if necessary for IHT reduction
Arrange Funeral list, name, emails, contact numbers

Post Will Objectives

Grant of Representation has been obtained,' How to obtain probate - a guide for the applicant acting without a solicitor' and more information is available from your local probate registry.

Notification of death to the deceased doctor, credit card companies, the Passport Office, clubs or societies, surrender of driving licences, shotgun or firearm certificates, transfer of insurance policies covering house, contents or motor cars into the names of the Personal Representatives or beneficiaries, completion of tax returns relating to liabilities arising prior to death.

Letters of Administration, An administrator is appointed by the court although he or she applies to the Probate Registry who then issue a sealed Grant of Representation in the name of the court.

Once provision has been made for the payment of debts and expenses, the Executors must consider payment of legacies.

Cash legacies are paid once the Executors are satisfied that they will not be required for payment of the estate debts and expenses.

Executors can also consider interim payments to beneficiaries who are entitled to what is left (the residue). They must ensure, however, that adequate provision is made for payment of debts and expenses,

Certificate of discharge and letter of confirmation, HMRC will issue a confirmatory letter stating that their enquiries are settled and that no tax is due, or that all tax has been paid or that all tax has been paid except that which is deferred. The effect of a letter is to release all persons, in particular the Executors from further liability to IHT unless there is deferred tax to pay and unless there is fraud or failure to disclose important facts.

The final step in the administration of the estate is likely to be the preparation of the statement of account for the residuary beneficiaries. The purpose of the account is to show all the assets of the estate, the payment of debts, administration expenses, income accrued, payments on account made and legacies paid and the balance remaining for the residuary beneficiaries. The balance will normally be represented by a combination of assets transferred to the beneficiaries in kind or cash. Approval of the accounts is shown by signature of the beneficiaries on the accounts releasing the Executors from further liability to the beneficiaries in the absence of fraud or failure to disclose assets.

Distribution Model Objectives

If a beneficiary has been left a house or other property then any outstanding debts and mortgage have to be addressed by the Executors to pay off the mortgage.

The house becomes the responsibility of the beneficiaries. Who can mortgage, lease, and sell the asset should all consent.
Transfer the property into your own name by contacting the Land Registry

Steady State Objectives

Prepare an update will, Lasting Power of Attorney, Pilot Trust

Conroy Ellis

Estate Project Plan

When completing this matrix please show the stages the project will now go through to achieve delivery. Start and end column should illustrate when you expect the stage to start and end. Milestones should be the major achievements expected, and the date that these are anticipated. You should also capture the major products (deliverables) that are planned as part of achieving each milestone.

We would recommend having one row per milestone, as these are key dates for the project.

Stage	Start and end	Milestones	Date	Other products to be produced

Risks & Issue Template

The Risk Register and Issue Log may be maintained separately, but the major risks and issues should be noted here.

Risk	Owner	Likelihood	Impact	Mitigation

Issue	Owner	Impact	Plan

Executor's lifecycle Process

Steps	General tasks	Project Process
-1	• Death certificate by your doctor • Interim certificate if coroner involved	• Start Up Ensure basis to start the project
-2	• Arrange Funeral	• Initiating Planning the event for Beneficiaries
-3	• Ensure valid and most recent last Will and Testament before acting, possibly advice needed by specialist solicitors • Executors or Personal Representatives identified • Fact finding exercise to ascertain the financial size and shape of the deceased's estate • Apply for Probate • Attendance at Probate Registry, swear the oath • If the estate more than nil rate band, Form 1HT 200 is the HMRC account for inheritance tax, completed by reference to form 1HT 210 guidance notes. • Grant of probate issued shortly, usually it takes two to three week to arrive from the Principal Registry in London • Executors role begin on behalf of beneficiaries	• Delivery The solution delivered to hand over to the Beneficiaries

	• Consider Deed of variation, to change the legal document for the purpose of Inheritance tax. Within two year of a death of the deceased. • Ensure an appropriate charging clause under the terms or the will in accordance with Trustee Act 2000	
-4	• Intestacy if no will means Letters of administration	• Delivery The solution delivered to hand over to the Beneficiaries
-5	• Contact all financial organisations where the decease has accounts and insurance polices • An professional tracing agency needed to locate beneficiaries worldwide	• Delivery The solution delivered to hand over to the Beneficiaries
-6	• Prepare paperwork to establish the net estate figure for HMRC • Apply for a Grant of Probate	• Delivery The solution delivered to hand over to the Beneficiaries
-7	• Pay all debt, liabilities, liquidate or settle assets • HMRC are first creditors where the following needs to paid • Inheritance Tax, Income Tax, Capital Gain Taxation	• Delivery The solution delivered to hand over to the Beneficiaries
-8	• Prepare Estate Accounts • Audited by Qualified Accountants if necessary	• Delivery The solution delivered to hand over to the Beneficiaries

| -9 | • Acquired Court to approve Estate Account | • Closure
The solution delivered to hand over to the Beneficiaries |
| -10 | • Distribute to Beneficiaries | • Closure
The solution delivered to hand over to the Beneficiaries |

Note: An Executor cannot be faulted if they choose to take professional advice

Project Controls

1. Checkpoint/Highlight report

The following information will be reported at the following regularity, to the specified groups, some examples have been given to help.

Information	Regularity	Audience
People/Staff utilisation	*Monthly*	
Milestones achieved		
Expenditure against plan		
Major achievements		
New risks or issues		

2. Approvals

Approvals will be sought for the following

Topic	Approver
External expenditure over £x	
Changes that affect the Milestone dates	
Changes that affect the product based planning	
Changes that affect the budget by more than 5%	
External communications affecting reputation	
Changes that affect the value of the benefits	

3. Stakeholder Register

Please use this table to record the stakeholders that will be affected by the project.

Individual or Group name	Organisation	Areas of interest	Level of impact	Positive or negative	Point of contact

4. Communications Plan

Please outline the major communications activities planned for the project.

Activity	Objective	Target audience	Channel	Originator	Date

Project Initiation Document

Scope

Outline the scope of the project and the areas that you will be addressing.

Out of scope

Confirm the areas that this project won't be addressing, which stakeholders might have expected you to be dealing and give the reasons for not addressing them.

Approach to delivery

Provide a summary of the approach to achieving the overarching objectives for the project

Resource profile

Please outline the resources (including the project team) that will be used for delivery of the project and how much of their time is anticipated to be used and when. Time window is the period during which they will be required.

Name	Role	Responsibilities and contribution	Anticipated time	Time window

5. Final Budget

This should be the summary of the expenditure. Please use High, Medium and Low on your confidence levels in the figure. In further information please note how you came to the figure, whether it could go up or down and any other options you have considered and rejected and why.

Expenditure Item	Estimate	How confident are you in the accuracy of this figure	Further information

6. Business Benefits

Provide a list of the benefits that will happen from this project. If there is no financial value, for example it is a social value benefit; please explain how it will be measured. The Level of confidence should be indicated as High, Medium or Low.

Use the "Dependency" column to describe what must happen to enable this benefit to occur, e.g. project deliverables, changes outside of the project, decisions etc.

Planned benefit	Financial Value	Dependency	How confident are you in this figure	How it will be measured	Business Owner

Lesson Learned Report

Good (What went well)

Description	Project Action	Impacts	Recommendation

Bad (What went bad)

Description	Project Action	Impacts	Recommendation

Improve (What can be done differently next time)

Description	Project Action	Impacts	Recommendation

Bibliography by Authors

Acland Floyer Andrew, Resolving disputes without going to court

Bennis, W., 1997. "Learning to Lead," Addison-Wesley, MA

Fisher, Ury and Patton, Getting to yes,

Honey Peter, Improve your people skills,

King Lesley, 6th Edition, Probate Practitioner's Handbook, Law Society Publishing

Knight Julian, Wills, Probate & Inheritance Tax for Dummies

Kor Rudy and Wijen Gert 50 Checklists for project and programme managers

Nass E Herbert, The 101 Estate Planning Mistakes

Norman: Parental Empathy. Parenthood, Little, Brown, NY.

Kouzes, J. M: "The Leadership Challenge," Jossey-Bass Publishers, CA.

Newton Richard, Brilliant Checklists for Project Managers, Prentice Hal

Richards Keith, Agile Project Management: Running PRINCE2 projects with DSDM Atern, The Stationary Office

Riddett Robin, King Lesley, Gausden Peter, Will Draftsman's Handbook

Scott Susan, Fierce Conversations

Steinhouse Robbie and West Chris Think like an Entrepreneur

Thompson Leigh, The Truth about Negotiation "You may want to make the first offer"

Thurston John, A Practitoner's Guide to Executorship and Administration, Tottel Publishing, Seventh Edition

Whitehouse Christopher, Lesley King, A Modern Approach to Wills, Administration and Estate Planning (with Precedents)

Young L Trevor, How to be a better project manager,

Contains public sector information licensed under the Open Government Licence v3.0", and to provide a link to the Open Government Licence

The Risk management self-assessment handbook, Ministry of Justice, 2010, licensed under the Open Government Licence v3.0.

Useful Websites

The following web pages are for information purpose

http://www.best-management-practice.com/successfulProjects2005_demo/content.aspx?page=p1_2&showNav=true&expandNav=false

http://www.slideshare.net/spouf/prince2-manual-3rd-edition-2002

http://www.thedailymind.com/how-to/how-to-deal-with-problem-family-members-without-losing-your-mind/

http://www.britishcouncil.org/learning_guide_-_negotiating_skills.pdf

http://www.desktoplawyer.net/dtl/index.cfm?event=base:article&node=A76991BD77118

http://www.thackraywilliams.com/probate-a-comprehensive-guide

http://www.whichlegalservice.co.uk

http://www.bcgwebdesign.co.uk/cafm/services/inheritance/how-to-approach-estate-planning/

http://www.bryant-thomas.com.au/tencommonmistakes.html

http://legaltechdesign.com/life-plan-project/2014/01/15/dont-have-a-will-10-common-but-misguided-excuses/

http://www.clsmoney.com/wills/

http://moorelawfirmllc.com/case-pages/estate-planning-and-wills-Moore-Law-Firm-LLC-Griffin-GA.html

Conroy Ellis

http://www.ehow.com/video_4961616_what-executor-compensation.html

http://bruceharrislaw.blogspot.com/

http://www.bcgwebdesign.co.uk/cafm/services/inheritance/how-to-approach-estate-planning/

Project Management Glossary

The terms and descriptions in this Glossary are taken from Managing Successful Projects with PRINCE2, Fifth edition Crown Copyright, 2009.

Acceptance

The process of accepting the delivery of a deliverable or product.

Activity

Any work performed on a project which uses resources (people, materials or facilities) has an associated cost and duration and results in one or more products/deliverables. Usually specified in a Work Breakdown Structure (WBS) and shown on a Gantt chart.

Actuals

What happens to a plan in real life.

A plan initially consists of forecasts for the work to be done and the resources to be used over a period of time. This can be measured in cost, in results, in time – in anything that was quantified in the original plan. Work never, or very rarely goes according to plan, and therefore a key aspect of project control is measuring the actuals against what was forecast and adjusting the plan accordingly.

Assumption

A statement that is taken for granted without concrete proof.

Assumptions are made during project planning and are used as a basis for estimating costs, duration and risk impact, etc. They should therefore be fully acknowledged and analysed by the Project Manager.

Baseline

A snapshot of a product and its constituent sub-products.

Once a deliverable/product has been formally accepted it becomes a baseline. A Configuration Librarian logs alterations to the baseline products/deliverables, enabling changes to be monitored. Baseline products normally have a version number associated with them. Baseline products such as software systems are permanently recorded so that they can be recalled at any time.

Budget

The amount of money allocated to the project. This often includes provisions for changes, risks and tolerance.

Business Case

The business justification for the project. The Business Case defines the expected benefits of the project, as well as how project success is to be measured.

Change control

Managing changes to baseline products/deliverables. On large projects this is a well-documented process involving many different stakeholders.

Change Control Board (CCB)

The group of stakeholders responsible for assessing changes to baseline products/deliverables. The Change Control Board must know why the change is needed and the expected impact on cost/time/quality/scope/risks and benefits. It is their decision to reject, adopt or adapt the proposed change. If change is accepted then new plans and estimates are developed and incorporated into baseline plans.

Change request

A proposal for alterations to a baseline product/deliverable.

Change requests are submitted to the Change Control Board, along with the results of the impact analysis.

Client

The people/organization who/which benefits most from project success. Also known as the customer. The client will see the project as helping them solve one or more business problems. The client pays for the project and will expect to see a return on its investment in the form of benefits.

Close out

Refers to the activities required to close the project, either because the project has come to the end of its lifecycle and has successfully delivered the products/deliverables it set out to deliver, or the project is being closed prematurely because it is no longer worthwhile continuing.

Concession

A deviation from the baseline project scope that is accepted by the project's senior decision-makers (Project Board or Steering Committee).

Constraints

Any restrictions to project timescales, budgets and resources.

Contingency

Time and resources set aside in the plan for dealing with risk events should they occur. This is often confused with slack which is put into a plan in case of delays in the schedule.

Controlling

Monitoring, evaluating, adjusting and reporting project progress.

This is where actuals are measured against what was originally projected. Corrective action may be taken to ensure that the project remains within its limits and to ensure that the product fulfils the necessary criteria.

Critical path

The sequence of dependent activities that will take the longest time to complete within the project. It is this longest sequence which determines the end date of the project. Critical path analysis allows the Project Manager to analyse the impact to the schedule caused by adjusting individual activities.

Customer

The person or group who commissioned the project.

Deliverable

A product that must be 'delivered' as part of the contractual obligations of the project. These are often the products which are handed over to the customer/user at the end of the project. The customer/user will then use them to realize benefits.

As well as final deliverables, this includes interim products such as plans, designs and reports.

Dependency

The relationship between two activities, when one cannot be started until the other is complete.

Effort

The amount of work required to perform an activity. This can be measured in 'person' hours (i.e. the amount of work which can be performed by one person in one hour), days, weeks, months or years. However, for planning purposes, activities are usually assigned in terms of person days.

End Project Report

Usually produced by the Project Manager at the end of a project. The End Project Report documents the overall project performance and any major issues that were raised.

Estimate

The prediction of measurable input or output, for example the cost or the duration of the project.

Impact

The effect of an issue or change on the project outcome or constraints.

Life cycle

The path from project conception to closure, defined by a set of distinct phases. In the PMBOK these are: conceive, define, start, perform and close.

Milestone

A significant event in the duration of a project, frequently the delivery of an important product. Milestones typically have zero duration and effort. For example: the production of five spare computer parts is an activity. The delivery of the computer parts is a milestone.

Mitigation

A series of actions intended to reduce the likelihood or impact of an anticipated risk.

Objectives

The desired outcomes of a project, measured in terms of deliverables as well as intangible benefits.

Phase

The set of activities leading up to project milestones. These are usually represented on the Work Breakdown Structure (WBS).

Planning

Determining how project objectives will be accomplished by identifying and organising the activities and resources necessary.

Project

A temporary structure set up with a duration, budget, scope and objectives.

Product

Any tangible output. A product may be a physical item, an item of software, an intellectual creation, a service or documentation. If a product is to be delivered as part of the contractual obligations of the project, then it is also a 'deliverable'.

Process

The series of steps required to accomplish a project activity.

Resources

The things (e.g. people, money, equipment) needed to complete the project.

Project management

The process of managing (planning, running, monitoring and controlling) a project.

Project Manager

The person responsible and ultimately accountable for a project's performance.

Project Plan

Defines the products required and the necessary activities, time, budget and resources.

The initial plan is typically high level, but as the project progresses more details can be added, so that the plan becomes more accurate in its estimated duration, cost and required resources.

Requirements

Formal statement of objectives, describing the features, functions and performance constraints to be delivered on the product.

Risk

A hypothetical event that might affect the successful outcome of a project.

Risk Management

The process of managing the risks associated with a project in order to minimise potential impact should the risk occur.

Schedule

Timeline identifying start/end dates for all project activities.

Scope

The full set of features and functions to be provided by the project.

Slippage

The variance between the planned and actual cost or schedule.

Stage

The division of the project into sections (stages) each stage forming a "go or no go" decision point. It is where the project's plans and Business Case is re-assessed to determine whether the project should continue.

Stakeholders

Anyone with an interest in the successful outcome of the project.

Task

Work done by staff over a period of time to produce deliverables. The same as "Activity."

Tolerance

The permissible deviation in plan which is allowed before bringing to the attention of the next level of management. Tolerances can be set for time, cost, benefits, scope, risk and quality. An example for time might be +10 days/-5 days on a forecasted deliver date of 15th June. This means that the Project Manager would be expected to deliver no earlier than 10th June (-5 days) and no later than 25th June (+10 days).

Work Breakdown Structure (WBS)

A hierarchical breakdown of the project activities.

The WBS is developed by a top-down decomposition of high-level activities into low-level activities. For example: "Create Project Management Glossary" might be broken down into "Select Project Management terms" and "Create definitions" etc.

Some common legal terms explained

Administrator

The person(s) appointed to distribute the estate if someone dies without a valid will or without appointing executors or if the appointed executor is unable or unwilling to act

Assets

Anything owned by the deceased, which together make up the gross value of an estate

Beneficiary

A person or persons who benefits from a will

Bequest

A term sometimes used instead of legacy

Capital Taxes

The office of HM Revenue and Customs that deals with the administration of Inheritance Tax

Chattels

Personal belongings, for example, jewellery, furniture, wine, pictures, books, and even cars and horses not used for business

Codicil

A separate document amending the terms of an existing will

Estate

All the assets of a person at the time of death

Executor

Person appointed to put into effect the terms of a will

Grant of Probate

The document issued by the probate registry to the executors of a will to authorise them to administer the estate

Intestate/Intestacy

When a person dies without a valid will they are said to be intestate. The estate is then distributed according to statutory regulations called the Rules of Intestacy.

Legacy

A gift under the terms of a will

Letters of Administration

Official acknowledgement by the Court of the appointment of administrators

Pecuniary Legacy

A fixed sum of money given by will

Personal Representative

Generic term for executors and administrators

Testator

A person who makes a will

Trust

A legal arrangement under which assets are looked after by trustees for the benefit of the beneficiaries upon a trust set out in the trust document or will

Trustee

A person responsible for administering a trust

Will

The document in which you say what is to happen to your possessions on your death

Accounting Glossary

Accounts

Financial statements prepared at the end of a period to reflect the profit of loss or the period and financial position at the end of the period.

Accounting period

Time period for which financial statements are prepared (e.g. month, quarter, year).

Accruals basis

The effects of transactions and other events are recognised when they occur (and not as cash or its equivalent is received or paid) and they are recorded in the accounting records and reported in the financial statements of the periods to which they relate (see also matching).

Assets

Something a person or business owns/uses, e.g. equipment or rights to a trademark.

Audit

An audit is the independent examination of, and expression of opinion on, financial statements of an entity.

Cash flow

Statements of cash expected to flow into and out of a business over a particular period.

Expense

Generally the running costs of a business.

Financial statements

Documents presenting accounting information which is expected to have a useful purpose, commonly known as 'the accounts'.

Forecast

Forecast estimate of future performance and position based on stated assumptions and usually including a quantified amount.

Profit

A financial benefit that is realized when the amount of revenue gained from a business activity exceeds the expenses, costs and taxes needed to sustain the activity. Any profit that is gained goes to the business's owners, who may or may not decide to spend it on the business.

Work-in-progress

Cost of partly completed goods or services, intended for completion and recorded as asset. Akin to stocks.

Index

A

Accounts 5, 6, 28, 30, 32, 35, 41, 66, 72, 97, 98

Accruals 28, 31, 97

Active 28, 40, 50

Activity 26, 63, 75, 85, 92

B

Beneficiaries v, 1, 3, 4, 6, 10, 16, 18, 21, 22, 27, 30, 32, 33, 35, 40, 42, 46, 47, 50, 52, 57, 60, 65, 66, 71, 73, 95

Benefits 5, 6, 10, 17, 19, 20, 56, 58, 60, 74, 78, 86, 88, 90, 92

Budget 25, 28, 29, 31, 34, 59, 60, 74, 77, 86, 90

Business Case 16, 19, 47, 56, 58, 60, 86, 92

C

Calendarisation Method 30

Change iv, 1, 12, 17, 19, 23, 25, 29, 32, 33, 47, 60, 72, 74, 79, 86, 89

Charging 7, 72

Clauses 7

Control vii, 13, 17, 19, 20, 22, 30, 31, 34, 40, 47, 50, 60, 74, 85, 86

Critical Path 26, 27, 88

Critical Success Factors 21, 58

D

Deed of Variation 19, 47, 72

E

Estate v, vii, viii, 1, 2, 4, 6, 9, 10, 12, 16, 19, 20, 22, 27, 30, 32, 33, 35, 39, 40, 42, 46, 50, 52, 60, 63, 64, 66, 69, 71, 73, 81, 82, 84, 93, 94

Estate Communication Plan 35, 46, 60, 69

Estimate 28, 30, 32, 77, 87, 89, 98

Executor iii, vii, ix, 1, 2, 5, 6, 9, 17, 19, 21, 22, 26, 30, 32, 33, 36, 40, 42, 46, 51, 55, 57, 59, 64, 66, 71, 74, 85, 93, 94

Executor Lifecycle Process 16, 36

F

Forecast 17, 28, 29, 31, 85, 98

G

Gift with reservation 3

I

Inheritance Tax 1, 2, 11, 23, 71, 81, 93

Intestacy 2, 72, 94

Issues 53, 63

L

Lawyer iv, vii, 10, 21, 39, 42, 48, 52, 58

Lesson Learnt Report 37, 79

Life Insurance Policies 3, 5

Listening 50

N

Negotiation 37, 48, 49, 82

Nil Rate Band 4, 11, 71

P

Potentially Exempt Transfer (PETS) 3

PRINCE2 v, 17, 81, 83, 85

Probate 1, 4, 23, 41, 42, 44, 65, 71, 81, 83, 94

Profile 28, 30, 31, 77

Project Board 17, 18, 19, 47, 53, 54, 61, 87

Project Initiation Document 16, 19, 76

Project Plan 19, 24, 29, 36, 63, 69, 91

R

Report 19, 26, 27, 35, 36, 37, 63, 64, 74, 81, 88, 89

S

Solicitors 71

Stakeholders 35, 56, 60, 75, 76, 86, 92

T

Task Report 26, 27, 36, 63

Taxation 5, 6, 17, 19, 27, 30, 35, 72

Testator 4, 18, 39, 51, 95

Trust 3, 4, 10, 11, 12, 14, 18, 22, 37, 44, 64, 67, 95, 97

Trustee 3, 6, 7, 10, 11, 19, 72, 95, 97

W

Will vii, 1, 2, 3, 4, 5, 6, 7, 9, 10, 12,
14, 15, 16, 17, 18, 19, 20, 21, 22,
24, 25, 26, 27, 28, 29, 30, 33,
35, 36, 37, 39, 40, 41, 42, 43,
44, 45, 46, 47, 48, 49, 51, 52, 57,
58, 59, 60, 63, 64, 65, 66, 67,
69, 71, 72, 74, 75, 76, 77, 78, 81,
82, 84, 87, 88, 90, 93, 94, 95, 97